COACHING
WITH
IMPACT

KEN ADAMS

Coaching with Impact
impactdisciples.com

Written by Ken Adams
Designed and Formatted by Grace Asnip
Edited by Elaine Meyer

FORWARD

As a former professional baseball player, I recall some of my former managers or coaches' famous last words before taking the field of competition. They stayed etched in my mind during the game, after the game, and after my playing career was over. The "last words" people speak make the most impact. Those people know their specific mission is ending. Their words carry great significance; whether entrusting a last will and testimony to family members, or exhorting athletes, teammates, or coaches to love each other as family and play together as a unit. In the heart of a person who is uttering his or her "last words," there is deep emotion and desire for those words to be followed and carried out.

One of the great mysteries of all times is how the Church and individual followers of Jesus Christ have rarely worked out the last words of Jesus into their daily lives, coaching lives, and Church lives. Jesus said, "All authority in heaven and on earth has been given to Me. Go therefore and make disciples of all nations, baptizing them in the Name of the Father and of the Son and of the Holy Spirit, teaching them to observe all that I have commanded you. And behold, I am with you always, to the end of the age."

The command embedded in these words is to make disciples. It is the "Great Commission," not the "Great Suggestion." However, Christians' track record of leading others to spiritual maturity and on to spiritual multiplication would suggest we have forgotten the very heart and words of Jesus as He returned to His

Father in heaven. To get more personal, the challenge we need to be laser focused on is whether or not we have grown to become a "fully trained" disciples who in turn make more fully trained disciples.

I have stood in locker rooms and coaches' rooms with head coaches and assistant coaches at all levels over the past thirty-one years as a Major League Baseball scout consistently asking one question, "How many of you have been discipled by someone who intentionally developed you into a fully trained follower of Jesus Christ?" Most coaches respond with, "No one has trained me." Why is it that Jesus' explicit command and clear commission have been set aside in our culture today? How can you as a coach begin to develop a disciple-making focus?

In *Coaching with Impact*, Ken Adams unpacks a clear biblical framework to becoming a fully trained disciple making coach. Coaching with Impact is designed for coaches to come alongside each other and help them leverage the influence God has given them. Leveraging your influence is not automatic. Every coach needs to grow and develop. They need to clearly understand their "why." They need to be equipped, trained, and challenged in how to "be" as a disciple of Christ and how to lead others to "build" more disciples of Christ. *Coaching with Impact* will challenge you to become more like Christ in your character and your conduct and less like yourself. Hopefully, who you are and what you do will become more like Christ and those changes will lead to becoming a disciple making coach who is coaching with impact.

Kevin Burrell
Area Scouting Supervisor
Chicago White Sox

INTRODUCTION

I've been involved in some form of organized athletics since I was five years old. I've played football, baseball, basketball, wrestled, and ran track. Basically, I spent my whole life in one of four places: home, school, church, or some form of sports field. Sports are in my blood, and my love for them runs deep.

In college I decided to get a degree in education with the plan to become a teacher and coach. That plan came to pass and I had the opportunity to coach for several years until God redirected my path. Two years into my coaching and teaching career God got my attention and called me to full-time vocational ministry. Upon graduation of seminary, I planted a church and have spent the past three decades coaching in the local church.

Even though today I am more of a spiritual coach than an athletic coach, my love for sports continues. I love watching sports, playing sports, and being around sports of all kinds. I also have a heart for coaches and believe that coaches are some of the most influential people on the planet. That is why I wrote *Coaching with Impact*.

With some encouragement from my friend and baseball scout, Kevin Burrell, I decided it was time to put some energy into helping coaches maximize their influence for Christ. I wrote this course to help coaches become disciples and disciple-makers. Kevin and I both believe that a movement of multiplying coaches is the very heart of God.

As you begin this course, let me give you some quick words of encouragement. Read your weekly lesson and commit to being at your small group for discussion. Also, make sure you complete the Weekly Workouts. The Weekly Workouts include a memory verse, daily readings from scripture, and questions for reflection and discussion. Each Weekly Workout also includes an activity that will help you apply the lesson to your life. Don't leave that activity out.

My prayer is that over the next twelve weeks you will have a better understanding of what being a disciple of Jesus Christ looks like and that you will also be committed to helping make more disciples of Christ. May God bless you as you begin learning what it means to coach with impact.

Being and Building,

Ken Adams

Coaching With Impact

Coaches have influence! All coaches have influence. Recreation league coaches have influence. Middle School and High School coaches have influence. College coaches have influence and Professional coaches have influence. Every coach has a certain level of influence both on and off the field or court. How a coach leverages this influence is critical.

Coaches can have positive or negative influence. We all know coaches that have a reputation for coming unglued and irate. There are coaches who yell at players, throw stuff across the room, and do things on and off the field that lack integrity. We also know coaches who have outstanding reputations. They are the right type of people, doing the right things, and doing them in the right way.

Coaches have influence with lots of different people. They have influence over players, parents, people in the community, as well as other coaches. Imagine what can happen when a coach uses their unique level of influence in a positive way to nudge people closer to God? A coach can have an impact in a way that many people will never have. Their character and their conduct can be displayed in a way that people all around them get better and become more like Christ. That is called coaching with impact!

The influence a coach has with players and other coaches is the reason for this book. *Coaching with Impact* was designed for coaches to come alongside each other and help them maximize the influence God has given them. A coach who maximizes his or her influence is not automatic. A coach needs help in becoming the person God wants them to be. They need to grow and develop. They need to be equipped and trained in how to live as a disciple of Christ and how to lead others to be disciples of Christ. Over the next several weeks in *Coaching with Impact* you will be challenged to become more like Christ in your character and conduct. Hopefully, who you are and what you do will become more like Christ and those changes will lead to a greater and more positive influence through your life.

More than likely you received a copy of this book because someone invited you to go through it with them. That's the goal of *Coaching with Impact*. Your influence grows as your character and conduct are shaped by the Word of God, the Spirit of God, and the People of God.

Over the next several months you will be in training. You will grow deeper in God's Word, study the character and conduct of Christ, and be encouraged and challenged to become the coach God has designed you to be. Once you complete the *Coaching with Impact* training the goal is to repeat it with another coach. Coaches helping coaches become more like Christ is the ultimate goal of this course.

GREAT COMMISSION COACHES

Let's be clear that the ultimate mission of every person on the planet is to be and build disciples of Christ. In Matthew 28:19,20 Jesus said, *"Go therefore and make disciples of all nations, baptizing them in the name of the Father and of the Son and of the Holy Spirit, teaching them to observe all that I have commanded you. And behold, I am with you always, to the end of the age."* These words are the marching orders for every single Christ follower. It does not matter if you're a coach, construction worker, business man, or housewife. The reason we are on this planet is to be the disciple God wants us to be and in turn help others become the disciple God wants them to be.

A coach that is coaching with impact understands that what they do on and off the field or court is simply a means to an end. The ultimate goal of coaching is to use sport as a means to the end of making disciples of all nations. Football, baseball, basketball, wrestling, soccer, lacrosse, golf and every other sport are simply the vehicles we use to connect with players and coaches and help them become fully trained disciples of Christ.

Remember, at the end of the day all that will matter is whether or not you have been a disciple and made more disciples. The number of games you win or lose will not matter in eternity. The trophies you have in the trophy case and the championship rings you wear will mean nothing after this life. All the holes in one you make and gold medals you obtain mean nothing on the other side of eternity. What will matter is how many disciples you have made! Jesus did not say, "*Go and make champions of all nations.*" He told us to make disciples who look and act like him.

It is important to perform at the highest level possible in whatever sport you are involved in. Doing your best is part of what it means to be a disciple. In fact, success increases the influence you will have. Your platform to use your influence will be greater the more successful you are. Poor performance does not increase your influence and it does not grow the platform you can use for God.

Just keep in mind that success simply enhances the level of influence you have for making more disciples. With great success comes greater opportunities to make disciples of Christ. Coaches who win the right way will always find themselves with more opportunities to share Christ and teach others to live for Christ. Coaching with impact means coaching at the highest level you possibly can, to have the greatest level of influence you can, for making disciples of Christ.

So, take a minute to think about your life. As a coach how well are you leveraging your influence for making disciples? Are you living your life as the disciple God created you to be? Are you using the platform God has blessed you with to influence others to be disciples of Christ. Are you coaching with impact?

The next several weeks are going to be a great opportunity for you to learn, grow, and evaluate your life as a coach. You will see how God can use your character and your conduct to impact athletes and coaches for the sake of Christ. Buckle up your chin strap and lace up your shoes; this is going to be a great opportunity for you to become the coach God created you to be.

WEEKLY WORK OUT: WEEK ONE

Main Takeaway: (Write down the one main takeaway you had from this week's lesson.)

_____

_____

_____

Memory Verse: (Matthew 28:19-20)

_____

_____

_____

Meditation: (Write down your thoughts on the verse of the day.)

Monday: (Ephesians 5:1)

_____

_____

_____

Tuesday: (John 13:15)

_____

_____

_____

Wednesday: (James 1:22)

_____

_____

_____

Thursday: (1 Corinthians 11:1)

_____

_____

_____

Friday: (Philippians 2:5)

_____

_____

_____

Making it Personal: (Answer the following questions for personal reflection.)

1- Has your influence as a coach been more negative or positive?

2- Do you feel like you have been more focused on the temporal or eternal rewards in your coaching?

Making it Practical: (Discuss the following questions with other members of your *Coaching with Impact* small group.)

1- Who are some coaches that have had an influence on your life? Describe how they influenced you.

2- Do coaches have a unique level of influence? Describe why or why you do not think this is true.

3- Read Matthew 28:19-20. Describe what it means to be a "Great Commission" coach.

4- How do you balance earthly success with eternal rewards?

Making it Stick: (Do the following action step in the next week.)
Send a note or text of thanks to a coach, teacher, or minister that
has had a positive influence on your life for Christ.

Fully Trained Coaches

Many Christians know the mission Christ has given us is to "make disciples of all nations". Most, however, do not know what it looks like when you make one. In Luke 6:40, Jesus makes it crystal clear: *"A disciple is not above his teacher, but everyone when he is fully trained will be like his teacher."* This means that the mission Christ has given us is to make disciples who resemble Him!

Just for a moment think how it would look if every coach was a "fully trained" coach. For that matter, imagine what a picture it would make if every believer was a "fully trained" disciple. If every coach and every believer were fully trained, that means they would have more of the character and conduct of Christ. If more people are more like Jesus, the world becomes a better place.

A world filled with people who have more Christlike character and conduct are better individuals, spouses, friends, employees, church members, and better citizens. The reason Jesus told us to make disciples of all nations is because it is his method for changing the world!

In *Coaching with Impact* our focus is simply to help coaches become fully trained disciples who have more of Christ's character and conduct. If it happens in the coaching world, the business world, the military world, the political world, the educational world, the arts and sciences, then eventually the world becomes a better place.

If the coaches in this small group become fully trained and in turn help more coaches become fully trained and so forth, then eventually it makes a dent in the darkness. This multiplication effect is exactly how Christ intended to change the world. When disciples make more disciples it multiplies and produces a world full of "fully trained" disciples. My challenge to you is to become a fully trained coach who is making more fully trained coaches and be part of changing the world.

CHRIST-LIKE CHARACTER AND CONDUCT

Character and conduct are the two things that display our likeness to Christ. Character can best be defined as "who you are" and conduct can best be defined as "what you do". When a coach is a "fully trained" disciple they are becoming more like Jesus in both character and conduct. The key word here is "becoming." No one ever arrives. We are in a process of becoming less like ourselves and more like Christ. That process is called sanctification. The original disciples were fully trained when Jesus handed over His mission to them, but they were never fully developed. We are not fully developed until we check into heaven. The goal is simply to keep growing and changing. As John the Baptist said in John 3:30, *"He must increase, but I must decrease."* Your character and conduct must become more and more like Christ's character and conduct.

Becoming more like Christ in your character and conduct is a result of the Word of God, the Spirit of God, and the people of God. As you learn more about Christ in His word, yield to the leading of His Spirit, and are challenged and encouraged by the people of God you will be transformed into the image of the Son of God.

A coach who is becoming more like Christ in who they are and what they do will be a coach with tremendous influence for Christ both on and off the field. A coach with Christ-like character will be a better person, a better spouse, a better parent, a better employee, a better church member, and a better member of the community. How can having more coaches that are fully trained be anything but good?

DEFINING CHRIST-LIKE CHARACTER

The character of Christ is not subjective, it is objective! We do not decide what Christ-like character looks like, God does. In Galatians 5:22-23 the Apostle Paul gave us a short and concise description of what Christ-like character looks like. *"But the fruit of the Spirit is love, joy, peace, patience, kindness, goodness, faithfulness, and self-control; against such things there is no law."* This list of spiritual fruit may not be all the ways to describe Christlike character, but all this fruit is true of Christ and should be more and more evident in each of us.

You do not need to guess what the character of Christ looks like. The Fruit of the Spirit makes it crystal clear. This means every fully trained disciple for the past two thousand plus years will be demonstrating more Christlike character. When a coach is demonstrating the character of Christ that means they are loving, joyful, peaceful, patient, kind, good, faithful, and self-control. How would that type of character not make any coach a better coach?

DEFINING CHRIST-LIKE CONDUCT

The conduct of Christ, like the character of Christ is not subjective, it is objective! In other words we do not pick and choose what we want to identify as Christ-like conduct or behavior. Jesus modeled His conduct clearly in the Gospel record. One can easily read through the Gospels and determine the things that Jesus did. However, there is an even more precise approach to defining the conduct of Christ.

Examining the conduct of the very first church, recorded in Acts chapter two, gives us a clear and concise picture of what the conduct of Jesus looked like. When you think about it, it actually makes perfect sense. The behavior of the Jerusalem Church would have been based on the conduct of the disciples and the conduct of the disciples was based on what they learned from being with Christ.

In Acts 2:42-47, the conduct of the Church in Jerusalem is described this way: *"And they devoted themselves to the apostles' teaching and the fellowship, to the breaking of bread and the prayers. And awe came upon every soul, and many wonders and signs were being done through the apostles. And all who believed were together and had all things in common. And they were selling their possessions and belongings and distributing the proceeds to all, as any had need. And day by day, attending the temple together and breaking bread in their homes, they received their food with glad and generous hearts, praising God and having favor with all the people. And the Lord added to their number day by day those who were being saved."*

What if every coach was doing what we see the disciples in the first church doing? What of every coach was belonging, growing, serving others and managing their resources to help others? What if every coach was worshipping and sharing the message of Jesus, and making more disciples? Coaches who demonstrate Christ-like conduct are without doubt influencers for Christ.

WHAT WE NEED TODAY

Without question we need more coaches today who look and act more like Christ. We need coaches who understand what it means to be fully trained and are committed to the process of becoming more like Christ. Now, more than ever, we need coaches with impact.

Multiplier · Member · Magnifier · Minister · Maturing · Manager · Messenger

Love   Goodness

Joy   Faithfulness

Peace   Gentleness

Patience   Self-Control

Kindness

WEEKLY WORK OUT: WEEK TWO

Main Takeaway: (Write down the one main takeaway you had from this week's lesson.)

_____
_____
_____

Memory Verse: (Luke 6:40)

_____
_____
_____

Meditation: (Write down your thoughts on the verse of the day.)

Monday: (Mark 3:14)

_____
_____
_____

Tuesday: (Acts 4:13)

_____
_____
_____

Wednesday: (John 20:21)

_____
_____
_____

Thursday: (Galatians 5:24)

_____

_____

_____

Friday: (Matthew 4:19)

_____

_____

_____

Making it Personal: (Answer the following questions for personal reflection.)

1- In what specific ways can your character be more like Christ's?

2- In what areas of Christlike conduct do see progress in your life and room for improvement?

Making it Practical: (Discuss the following questions with other members of your *Coaching with Impact* small group.)

1- Name a coach in your life that had outstanding character and how that impacted you.

2- Read Luke 6:40. What is a fully trained disciple and how is that different from fully developed?

3- Which Fruit of the Spirit could be more on "display" in your life?

4- Read Acts 2:42. Which behaviors in this passage would you like to develop in your life today?

Making it Stick: (Do the following action step in the next week.) Write out the Fruit of the Spirit from Galatians 5:22-23 and evaluate how well they are displayed in your life currently.

The Basics

A well-worn story tells of Vince Lombardi addressing the Green Bay Packers after suffering a humiliating loss. He held up a football in his hand and said, "Men this is a football." Lombardi was obviously telling his team it was time to get back to the basics.

Every coach knows the importance of mastering the basics. The basics are important in athletics as well as in disciple making. If we don't get the basics down, the chances of everything else working are slim to none. In order to maximize your influence for Christ it is imperative that you nail down a few spiritual basics.

THE BASICS OF SALVATION

Clearly the most important basic in Christianity is having salvation through a personal relationship with Jesus Christ. Until a person knows that they are saved and secured in Christ nothing else matters. Desiring Christ-like character and conduct apart from a saving relationship with Christ means absolutely nothing.

Salvation in Christ is what connects a person to God. Sin separates a person from God and faith in Christ connects a person to God. A person must believe and put their faith in Jesus Christ. Paul states it this way in Romans 10:9, *"If you confess with your mouth that Jesus is Lord and believe in your heart that God raised him from the dead, you will be saved."*

Have you nailed down the basic of salvation? Do you know that you know that you have surrendered your life to Christ and accepted His forgiveness and salvation from your sin condition? If not, then make that decision today and secure the issue of salvation once and for all. You can't earn your salvation. You cannot be good enough for salvation. You cannot buy your salvation. Salvation comes only through faith in God's grace.

THE BASICS OF BAPTISM

Biblical water baptism is a basic step of obedience in following Christ. This act of publicly professing faith in Jesus is a prerequisite for many other levels of obeying Christ. You are not very likely to pursue Christlike character and conduct if you are ashamed to publicly acknowledge you are devoted and committed to following Jesus. Baptism does not save you, but it is an important step in following Jesus and letting the world know that you belong to Him. Jesus tells us in Matthew 28:19 to *"... make disciples of all nations, baptizing them."*

Have you taken the step of biblical baptism? In the scriptures baptism always occurs after a person's salvation and by immersion. This is a great picture of what Christ has done for us. Baptism by immersion is a true representation of Christ's death, burial, and resurrection. If you have never taken the step of baptism you might consider undertaking that basic step of obedience as soon as you can.

THE BASICS OF CHURCH INVOLVEMENT

God has created the idea of church to be an environment for spiritual growth and a movement of believers to help accomplish Christ's mission. The church is literally a place where you can learn how to be a disciple and a place where you can work with others to build disciples. The church is designed to be a place where the Great Commandment and Great Commission can become a reality. The church is God's chosen vessel to help bring about change in the world.

Being actively involved in a local church is in many ways just as important as having a physical family to be involved in. The church really is a spiritual family for a Christ follower. It is the place where you are fed, where you learn, where you serve, and where you are disciplined, if necessary. It is really important for every believer to be actively involved in a local church for the sake of spiritual development and to be part of fulfilling Christ's mission.

I hope you have identified with a local bible-believing church as your spiritual family. If not, let me encourage you to take this important basic step of discipleship. A solid bible teaching fellowship that is on mission for God is the perfect place for you to become a person who can influence the world for Christ. Make a commitment to belong to a local church. Resist the urge to jump around from church to church and never plant yourself in a place where you can be known and accountable.

MASTERING THE BASICS

Christ's mission of making disciples of all nations requires going, baptizing, and teaching. Those three steps comprise the basics every believer needs. Salvation, baptism, and church involvement set you up for being a person, or coach, who makes an impact on the world for Christ. Be sure you master the basics to become the person God has created you to be.

WEEKLY WORK OUT: WEEK THREE

Main Takeaway: (Write down the one main takeaway you had from this week's lesson.)

_____

_____

_____

Memory Verse: (Acts 2:41-42)

_____

_____

_____

Meditation: (Write down your thoughts on the verse of the day.)

Monday: (John 3:3)

_____

_____

_____

Tuesday: (Ephesians 2:8-9)

_____

_____

_____

Wednesday: (Matthew 3:13)

_____

_____

_____

Thursday: (Matthew 16:18)

_____

_____

_____

Friday: (Ephesians 1:22-23)

_____

_____

_____

Making it Personal: (Answer the following questions for personal reflection.)

1- Are each of the basics in this lesson true about you or are there some things still missing?

2- How would you describe your current church involvement?

Making it Practical: (Discuss the following questions with other members of your *Coaching with Impact* small group.)

1- Regardless of the subject, how important are the basics and why are they important?

2- Read Acts 2:41-42. How are the basics of spiritual growth demonstrated here and why were they important at that time?

3- What are some of the common obstacles to the basics of salvation, baptism, and church involvement?

4- Read Hebrews 10:24. How does a good church environment help make this verse true in your life?

Making it Stick: (Do the following action step in the next week.) Have a conversation with your group leader about how each of the basics applies to your life personally.

Coaches With Christ-like Character

If three different people; a member of your family, a fellow church member, and a player from your team were asked to describe your character what would they say? Would they say things like-they are "a hot head", "demanding", "tough to deal with", "insensitive", "pushy", "over the top"? If these, or any similar descriptions, are how you are described it might be a sign that your character needs an overhaul. If on the other hand you are described as loving, joyful, peaceful, patient, kind, good, faithful, gentle, and self-controlled then you are actually demonstrating Christlikeness in your character.

As mentioned earlier, character is who you are, not what you do. Character is who you are on the inside. Character is the real you and it is usually demonstrated most in the way you relate to the people in your life. Contrary to some, a coach can have Christlike character. A coach with Christlike character can be very competitive and still demonstrate the character of Jesus in the way they treat people.

The character of Christ is not a random list of traits that can never be developed in our lives. The character of Christ is actually very subjective and it can best be summarized in the words of Paul found in Galatians 5:22-23. Paul said, *"But the fruit of the Spirit is love, joy, peace, patience, kindness, goodness, faithfulness, self-control; against such things there is no law."* This list of spiritual fruit is not a comprehensive description of Christ's character but it is a good summary of the character the Holy Spirit wants to produce in every believer.

A coach who is described as loving, joyful, peaceful, patient, kind, good, faithful, and self-controlled can be very competitive, a winner, and a great leader all at the same time. A coach with impact is a coach who fleshes out the fruit of the Spirit in their life both on and off the field. Let's take a closer look at each aspect of the Fruit of the Spirit and what it looks like inside a coach.

Love: The Bible tells us that God is love and that God loves us so much that He sent His one and only Son as a sacrifice so we could have eternal life. There is no better example of love than Jesus. Jesus embodies the character trait of love like no one else. Jesus loved His father. Jesus loved His disciples. Jesus loved His enemies. Jesus loves us!

When the Holy Spirit produces the fruit of love inside you it changes the way you treat people. Love isn't just a warm, fuzzy feeling. Love is an act of the will which causes you to sacrifice your agenda for others and to put them ahead of your own agenda. Love is a commitment we make. Love is active, it is something you do. Love is unconditional with no strings attached. Love is a command from God. We are commanded to love God and commanded to love people.

The Bible tells us in Romans 5:8, *"But God shows his love for us in that while we were still sinners, Christ died for us."* Imagine that! God demonstrated His love unconditionally and sacrificially even while we were still in sin and disobedience to Him. The Bible also tells us in John 13:35, *"By this all people will know that you are my disciples, if you have love for one another."* Love is the sign by which the world will know that we are disciples of Christ.

Coaching with impact means coaching with love. It means having a care and concern for the players and coaches around you that causes you to put them first and care about them as individuals. It means being willing to sacrifice for others and treating them the way Jesus would.

Joy: Many people confuse joy with happiness. Happiness is conditional. If I give you $10,000 dollars it will probably make you happy but not necessarily give you joy. On the other hand, you could lose $10,000 and still have a sense of joy inside. Joy is an inner contentment that comes from the presence of the Holy Spirit in your life.

While Paul was in prison he said in his Letter to the Philippians, *"Rejoice in the Lord always: again I will say rejoice."* Even in prison Paul was experiencing an inner sense of contentment. I assure you he was not happy about being in prison, but he was content because of the Holy Spirit's presence in his life. Joy is a condition of the heart and mind that is focused on God rather than the circumstances you find yourself in.

In coaching, as in all of life, it is easy to get caught in the trap of looking to your circumstances to bring you joy. Joy does not come in success or the lack of it. Joy comes from being in the center of God's will and being controlled by the Holy Spirit. One of the keys to life is learning to let the indwelling presence of the Holy Spirit bring you joy.

Peace: Peace is not the absence from the storms, but calm in the midst of the storms. The word for peace in the Greek language is "eirene" which means harmony. The peace that the Holy Spirit produces in your life is a peace that passes human understanding and logic. It is a calm inside when everything on the outside is chaos. This peace can only come from God's presence inside your life. The prophet Isaiah said, *"You keep him in perfect peace whose mind is stayed on you, because he trust in you."*

When you stay focused on the Lord and keep your thoughts centered on Him you will have a peace that cannot come from anywhere else. This peace will help you handle the stress that arises from circumstances that would otherwise create anxiety and worry. The Holy Spirit will produce inside you the same peace that Jesus had even when He knew the cross was in front of Him.

Think about the difference God's peace can make in the life of a coach. Coaching can be incredibly stressful so imagine how powerful it would be to have peace in a profession that is filled with turmoil. That type of peace does not come from the something you do, it comes from something God does in you! Let the

Holy Spirit control you and His peace will be with you in the midst of everything you do.

Patience: Every coach on the planet needs patience. Waiting for an athlete to develop or a team to win is a dilemma that every coach in history has dealt with. The Greek word for patience is *makrothumia,* which is sometimes translated "long-temper". What coach does not need a long temper?

The challenge in developing patience is that God teaches us patience by placing us in circumstances that make us wait. God uses exact opposite situations to produce in us the fruit of His Spirit. Just think about the patience Jesus showed with His team. Over and over again Jesus' patience was stretched thin when His disciples didn't progress as quickly as He wanted. However, Jesus did not give up on His disciples and He practiced patience in their development.

James 1:3 tells us, *"The testing of your faith produces steadfastness."* Steadfastness is another way of describing patience. As we allow the Holy Spirit to control us He provides the patience we need to pass the tests that come our way. Coaching with impact means being able to stay patient when people and circumstances are not going your way.

WEEKLY WORK OUT: WEEK FOUR

Main Takeaway: (Write down the one main takeaway you had from this week's lesson.)

_____

_____

_____

Memory Verse: (Galatians 5:22-23)

_____

_____

_____

Meditation: (Write down your thoughts on the verse of the day.)

Monday: (Romans 5:8)

_____

_____

_____

Tuesday: (Philippians 4:4)

_____

_____

_____

Wednesday: (Isaiah 26:3)

_____

_____

_____

Thursday: (Proverbs 16:32)

_____

_____

_____

Friday: (Proverbs 11:17)

_____

_____

_____

Making it Personal: (Answer the following questions for personal reflection.)

1- What would the three people mentioned in the first paragraph say at your funeral if it were today?

Making it Practical: (Discuss the following questions with other members of your *Coaching with Impact* small group.)

1- Describe the difference between character being subjective or objective.

2- Read John 13:35 and explain what love looks like in the world of athletics or coaching.

3- What is the difference between joy and happiness and how does it apply to the coaching role?

4- Read James 1:3. How does the Holy Spirit produce Christlike character in us?

Making it Stick: (Do the following action step in the next week.)
Plan an action that demonstrates the love of Christ and commit to
doing it this week.

Coaches With Christ-like Character Continued

In the previous lesson we looked at the first four aspects of the Fruit of the Spirit. The Fruit of the Spirit serves as a summary of what Christ-like character looks like inside of a fully trained disciple. A coach who has this type of character is a coach who can have great influence. Take a minute and re-read Galatians 5:22-23.

Kindness: Jesus would be the perfect picture of kindness. Used 80 times in the scriptures, the Greek word for kindness is *chrestotes* which means tender concern or uprightness. Solomon says in Proverbs 21:21, *"Whoever pursues righteousness and kindness will find life, righteousness, and honor."* Every coach ought to be a coach who pursues kindness in the way they treat others.

Just think about some of the ways Jesus demonstrated kindness. After a woman was caught in adultery Jesus demonstrated kindness while others were looking to stone her. The Bible tells us that Jesus had compassion on the crowds and saw them as sheep without a shepherd. One of Christ's most popular stories is a story of a Samaritan that demonstrated kindness to a man who was neglected and overlooked by others. No one can study the life of Christ and not see kindness as a character trait of His life.

Our world needs coaches who demonstrate kindness. The rough, tough, "mean" persona that some coaches display is not the character of a coach who has true influence and impact. Jesus would never be considered weak. He was a "man's man" and He was kind. Jesus treated people the right way and we need coaches that treat players and other coaches the same way Jesus treated people.

Goodness: The word goodness is used over 1000 times in scripture. It carries the meaning of treating people the right way. Goodness is defined in the dictionary as excellent or virtuous. When the Holy Spirit is in control of your life, goodness is the fruit that is produced through you. This Christlike character trait makes a difference in the way you treat others and in the amount of impact you may have in someone's life.

Jesus calls us to treat everyone with goodness, even our enemies. Every act of goodness is a sign to others of God's presence in your life and a way of glorifying Him. In Matthew 5:16, Jesus said, *"In the same way, let your light shine before others, so that they may see your good works and give glory to your Father who is in heaven."* When a coach acts and reacts with goodness, rather than anger or bitterness they are demonstrating a life that is filled with the Spirit of God. This kind of lifestyle points people to God and brings Him glory.

Coaches can demonstrate the goodness of God in so many different ways. It really just comes down to the condition of one's heart. Luke 6:45 says, *"The good person out of the good treasure of his heart produces good, and the evil person out of his evil treasure produces evil, for out of the abundance of the heart his mouth speaks."* Heart really represents a person's desires and motivation. When the heart is controlled by Christ it is easy to do good to others. When the heart is wrong the character will be flawed.

Faithfulness: Faithfulness is a dying characteristic in the world in which we live. People bail on just about everything and anything. They bail on marriage, they bail on family, they bail on churches, they bail on friends, they bail on jobs, and they bail on teams. It is a rare thing these days to find someone who sticks with a commitment they have made for the long haul.

It is a good thing that we serve a God who never bails. He will never leave us or forsake us. Deuteronomy 7:9 says, *"Know therefore that the Lord your God is God, the faithful God who keeps his covenant and steadfast love with those who love him and keep his commandments, to a thousand generations."* Godly character is character that demonstrates faithfulness to others the same way God demonstrates it to us.

A coach who is faithful is a coach who is true to his word. He or she does what they say they will do. They are known to be reliable and trustworthy. They can be counted on and are dependable. Faithful coaches show up and bring the best they have each and every time. They stay true to the *team* and to the *task* they are assigned to.

One way to understand the importance of faithfulness is to consider our own expectations. We expect our mail to be delivered. We expect our hot water heater to work. We expect our vehicle to start. We expect our spouse to be loyal.

A fellow coach, player on your team, and others expect a coach to show up when they are supposed to and be true to the role of a coach. This is true in every level of coaching, from recreational leagues to professional. A faithful coach is attractive to everyone, everywhere. We all want to play for a coach who demonstrates faithfulness.

Gentleness: In my experience the words "gentle" and "coach" don't typically go together, but they should. A coach does not have to be weak to be gentle. You can be "hard nose" and "tough as nails" and still have a gentle spirit that treats people the right way. A player can be aggressive on the field or court and still be gentle in the way they approach and relate to others.

No one on the planet was stronger than Jesus, yet He was the perfect picture of gentleness. Jesus was both tender and tough. Jesus never backed down from a difficult situation but He never allowed difficulties to make Him something or someone He was not. In 1 Timothy 6:11, spiritual leaders are described this way, *"But as for you, O man of God, flee these things. Pursue righteousness, godliness, faith, love, steadfastness, gentleness."* I believe those same traits are important for coaches to have. Coaches who do the right things and treat people the right way have a far greater chance to bring about positive influence on players than those who display the opposite traits.

A great picture of gentleness would be a wild horse verses a tame one. No one would argue that horses have strength and power. A tame horse, however, has that power under control and a wild one can be unpredictable and explosive. A person or coach who is gentle is a person that has strength and power but allows the Spirit of God to have control and uses that strength and power in the right way.

Self-Control: Strangely enough, when the Holy Spirit is in control, He enables you bear the fruit of self-control. In other words, the Holy Spirit's control is what enables you to demonstrate self-discipline. You can say "no" to temptation because the Holy Spirit gives you self-control. You can say "yes" to the right things because the Holy Spirit gives you the power to do so.

Jesus is a great example of demonstrating self-control. When Jesus was being tempted in the wilderness, He exercised self-control. When He ran the money changers out of the temple, He exercised self-control. When Jesus went to the cross, He exemplified self-control. Again and again, Jesus is demonstrating the ability to do what He might not have felt like doing. Jesus could get up early in the morning to meet with His Father because He had self-control.

Sometimes we have images of coaches screaming at players, throwing chairs, and breaking baseball bats. We see videos of coaches yelling at umpires and kicking benches and water coolers. We've all seen a coach slam a clip board or throw a glove. Sometimes we hear news stories of a coach being arrested for driving under the influence. All of the above are examples of coaches that are out of control because they lack the fruit of self-control. If you allow the Holy Spirit to be in control, he will empower you to exercise self-control.

HOW FRUIT IS PRODUCED

In John 15:4 Jesus says, *"Abide in me, and I in you. As the branch cannot bear fruit by itself, unless it abides in the vine, neither can you, unless you abide in me."* Christ's words remind us that spiritual fruit is not produced by self effort. Trying harder will not give you more love, joy, peace, or patience. Working at it will not make you kinder, gentler, or more faithful. Staying connected to Jesus and allowing His life to live through you is what produces fruit. The vine produces fruit, not the branch. The fruit simply needs to stay connected to the vine. I encourage you to learn what it means to abide in Christ. Remain in Christ's Word, allow His Word to remain in you, and you will see the Fruit of the Spirit produced in your life.

WEEKLY WORK OUT: WEEK FIVE

Main Takeaway: (Write down the one main takeaway you had from this week's lesson.)

_____

_____

_____

Memory Verse: (John 15:5)

_____

_____

_____

Meditation: (Write down your thoughts on the verse of the day.)

Monday: (Philippians 2:5)

_____

_____

_____

Tuesday: (James 3:17)

_____

_____

_____

Wednesday: (Exodus 34:6)

_____

_____

_____

Thursday: (Proverbs 25:28)

_____

_____

_____

Friday: (Isaiah 26:3)

_____

_____

_____

Making it Personal: (Answer the following questions for personal reflection.)

1- Which on of the fruit mentioned in this lesson challenges you the most?

2- In what area of life do you need self-control the most today?

Making it Practical: (Discuss the following questions with other members of your *Coaching with Impact* small group.)

1- Who comes to your mind when you think of some one is kind, good, and faithful?

2- Read Matthew 5:16. Why is it so important to demonstrate the character of Christ in front of others?

3- Why is demonstrating self-control such a challenge in the role of coaching?

4- Read John 15:4. What does it mean to abide in the vine and bear much fruit?

Making it Stick: (Do the following action step in the next week.) Demonstrate an act of kindness in a practical and tangible way in this coming week.

Coaches With Christ-like Conduct

A coach with impact is a coach who demonstrates the conduct of Christ in their life. Their behavior, what they do on and off the field is determined by the way Jesus lived. As 1 John 2:6 puts it in referring to Jesus, *"Whoever says he abides in him ought to walk in the same way in which he walked."* A coach who makes an impact is a coach who walks the same way Jesus walked.

Becoming a coach who has Christlike conduct is being a coach who models the behavior and actions of Christ. As Paul said in 1 Corinthians 11:1, *"Be imitators of me, as I am of Christ."* Paul sought to do what Jesus did. His goal was to live like Jesus lived and to be like Christ. Likewise, a coach that seeks to live like Jesus lived and to be like Christ is a coach who makes an impact.

Paul put it like this in 2 Timothy 2:2, *"and what you have heard from me in the presence of many witnesses entrust to faithful men, who will be able to teach others also."* In this verse you see multiple generations of disciples who are all following Jesus. What Paul taught Timothy he had learned from Christ. Timothy was teaching faithful men to teach the same things his own teacher, Paul, had learned from Jesus. The point here is that conduct is reproducible.

I believe one of the best ways to clearly see the conduct Christ wants us to live out in our lives today is by examining the behaviors of the disciples in the Jerusalem church. These disciples were modeling the behavior of the disciples who were modeling the behavior of Jesus. We need disciples today who are modeling the same conduct or behaviors of Christ that were being modeled two thousand years ago. When we have coaches that are modeling Christlike conduct imagine the potential that creates for impact the world!

In the earliest days of the first church in Jerusalem we see them being describe by the following marks of a disciple.

Belonging: In Acts 2:42 the disciples are described as *"devoted".* This devotion was an indication of commitment to Christ and to one another. They had several things in common. They had all received the word and accepted Christ. They had all been baptized. They were all devoted to involvement in the movement of Christ. Belonging to Christ and His Church was one of the first conducts or behaviors we see in the Jerusalem church. You can belong to the mission and movement of Jesus and not be a disciple but if you are a disciple you will certainly belong to the mission and movement of Christ.

A coach who makes on impact is a coach who is a committed member of a local body of Christ. He or she understands the propriety and value of belonging and has made it a conduct of their lifestyle. They are living like Jesus lived.

Growing: In Acts 2:42 the disciples were committed to the *"apostles teaching".* The apostles' teaching was the teaching of Jesus. They were simply teaching what Jesus had taught them. They were growing and maturing as they continued to learn the teachings of Christ.

Clearly, learning and growth are a behavior of every generation of disciples. Disciples of Jesus truly are life long learners and the two things they never stop learning are the character and conduct of Christ. You can be a student of scripture and not be a disciple, but if you are a disciple you will certainly be a student of scripture.

Coaches who impact others around them are coaches who are maturing spiritually. They have the conduct of learning and growth established in their lives and are consistently growing their knowledge and experience with Christ.

Serving: Acts 2:44 tells us, *"And all who believed were together and had all things in common."* The first church had all things in common because they cared about each other and were committed to serving one another. They knew each other's needs and were committed to meeting them. The first church was characterized by servanthood because they had seen it modeled in Christ.

Serving in the first church was a normal behavior among disciples. They all knew about Jesus washing the disciples' feet and they knew that they were called to treat each other the same way. Mark 10:45 was a constant reminder to them that, *"The Son of Man came not to be served but to serve, and to give his life as a ransom for many."* A disciple who did not serve was a contradiction in the first church and still is today.

A coach who makes an impact on the people in their sphere of influence are coaches who understand disciples are servants. They live with the conduct of serving, rather than being served in their day-to-day conduct.

Managing: The believers in Jerusalem learned how to manage their God-given resources to honor God and help others. Acts 2:45 says, *"They were selling their possessions and belongings and distributing the proceeds to all, as any had need."* These early disciples had discovered all they had (time, money, body, and relationships) was given by God to be used for His purposes. As stewards of the things that God had entrusted to them they managed it in a way that honored God and blessed others.

A person can be a great life manager and not be a disciple, but every disciple will be committed to growing into a better life manager. They will want to honor God with their time, money, body, and relationships. They understand that all they have was a gift by God to be used for God's glory. All of our resources are simply on loan and are given to us so that we can use them to accomplish the mission of Christ. If you are a fully trained disciple you will always be growing as a manager of life's resources.

A coach who knows everything they have ultimately belongs to God will manage it in a way that honors God. Coaches who see their resources as gifts entrusted to them by God to be used for Him are coaches that God can use to impact the world.

So far, we have taken a look at the first four marks of conduct found in a fully trained disciple. Before at looking a a few more, take some time to process what you have learned. Are these things true of your life? Where are these actions or behaviors strongest or weakest in your life? What steps do you need to take to grow in any of the behaviors that are lacking in your life?

WEEKLY WORK OUT: WEEK SIX

Main Takeaway: (Write down the one main takeaway you had from this week's lesson.)

_____

_____

_____

Memory Verse: (1 Corinthians 11:1)

_____

_____

_____

Meditation: (Write down your thoughts on the verse of the day.)

Monday: (Psalm 24:1)

_____

_____

_____

Tuesday: (Matthew 25:14)

_____

_____

_____

Wednesday: (Colossians 2:6-7)

_____

_____

_____

Thursday: (1 Peter 4:10)

_____

_____

_____

Friday: (Galatians 6:10)

_____

_____

_____

Making it Personal: (Answer the following questions for personal reflection.)

1- How would you rate the first four marks of Christlike conduct in your life currently?

Making it Practical: (Discuss the following questions with other members of your *Coaching with Impact* small group.)

1- Take a minute and explain the difference between character and conduct. Why are both important in the life of a coach?

2- Why was "belonging" an important part of the Church in Jerusalem? Do you believe "belonging" is important today?

3- What does being "devoted to the apostles' teaching" look like today?

4- Read Matthew 10:45. How does the conduct of serving look in the life of a disciples today?

5- Would you describe yourself as an ideal manager of your life today? Why or why not?

Making it Stick: (Do the following action step in the next week.) Read Acts 2:41-47 and evaluate your life according to the conduct of the believers in Jerusalem.

Coaches With Christ-like Conduct Continued

We finished the last lesson by looking at four marks of conduct found in Christ and the disciples of Christ. Let's take a few minutes to complete our study of the marks of conduct that are reproducible and transferrable in the life of every disciple and every disciple-making coach.

Worshipping: A fully trained disciple is a disciple who is marked by a lifestyle of worship. They magnify God in their life continually. They make it a priority to have times of personal worship and public worship as expressions of this 24/7 lifestyle. In the same way Jesus had private and personal times with the Father, they have private and personal times with the Father. In the same way Jesus went to the synagogue regularly, they go to public worship regularly. In Acts 2:46 the disciples *"attended the temple together."* The temple was their place of public worship much like a church is our place for public worship.

Gathering for corporate worship with other believers was not optional for a disciple. It was necessary. The gathering together for worship breathed life into the first disciples. It encouraged them and it energized their faith. They desperately needed to worship in the temple courts and it was a witness to others as they gathered.

When a coach makes a commitment to personal and public worship in their life it strengthens them personally and it witnesses to others. A person can be a worshipper and not be a fully trained disciple, but every fully trained disciple will be a devout worshipper.

Impact coaches are coaches who worship. They magnify Christ in a consistent time of personal worship and public worship. These expressions of worship are vitals parts of strengthening their faith and building their spiritual muscle.

Sharing: A fully trained disciple demonstrates the conduct of sharing their faith. They are messengers of the gospel. They look for opportunities to connect with people who are far from God and share with them how to be reconciled to God. In Acts 2:47 the disciples in the Jerusalem church were, *"praising God and having favor with all the people. And the Lord added to their number day by day those who were being saved."* People sharing Christ and people coming to faith in Christ was a normal thing in the church in Jerusalem. Daily people were coming to know Christ because the disciples were sharing Him.

The disciples in Jerusalem were messengers because Jesus was a messenger. Luke 19:10 describes Jesus this way, *"For the Son of Man came to seek and to save the Lost."* You cannot be a fully trained disciple who looks and acts like Jesus and not be a messenger.

Coaches have an incredible opportunity to be messengers for Christ. They often have open doors to share Christ with players, parents, and other coaches. They can be messengers with the gospel to people who might not be open to hearing the message from pastors and ministers. The athletic arena is a great place to share the message of Christ.

An impact coach is a coach who prays for and takes advantage of opportunities to speak up for Christ. They know what they do and what they say can be a powerful tool in communicating the message of Jesus. Impact coaches don't want to miss opportunities to share the greatest message in history.

Reproducing: In Acts 6:7 the church is described this way, *"And the word of God continued to increase, and the number of the disciples multiplied greatly in Jerusalem, and a great number of the priests became obedient to the faith."* The church was multiplying because the disciples were reproducing more and more disciples.

The disciples in Jerusalem took seriously Christ's words given on a mountainside in Galilee to *"make disciples of all nations"*. They were committed to becoming a movement of multiplication, not simply a movement of addition. They made disciples who in turn made more disciples. They were obedient to the commission that Jesus had given them.

What if today we could say, *"And the word of God continued to increase, and the number of disciple-making coaches multiplied greatly around the world"?* That is the goal. God wants a world full of coaches, teachers, business men, law enforcement officers, construction workers, and the list goes on of men and women who are proven multipliers of disciples. That is how we are going to change the world!

A coach who makes an impact is a coach who is reproducing or multiplying more disciples of Christ. It might be with other coaches, with players, or with anyone else the Lord brings into your life. The point is to multiply by making a disciple who makes another disciple. If we live life as multipliers there is no doubt God will use our influence and impact to transform others.

HOW BEHAVIOR IS TRANSFORMED

Christlike conduct is not the result of self-effort. It is the result of allowing the Holy Spirit to transform you. It is the result of allowing Christ to live his life through you. In Mark 3:14 Jesus transformed His disciples by being *"with Him."* Today, Jesus transforms His disciples by being *"in them."* As you die to self and allow the Holy Spirit to have control of you, He transforms you into the image of Christ. He transforms your conduct into the conduct of Christ.

The Holy Spirit makes you a member, a magnifier, a maturing disciple, a minister, a manager, a messenger, and a multiplier. The by product of the Spirit's control in your life is a life that looks like the disciples in Jerusalem, the original disciples of Jesus, and like Jesus Himself. That is what it means to be a fully trained disciple of Christ.

WEEKLY WORK OUT: WEEK SEVEN

Main Takeaway: (Write down the one main takeaway you had from this week's lesson.)

_____

_____

_____

Memory Verse: (Ephesians 5:1)

_____

_____

_____

Meditation: (Write down your thoughts on the verse of the day.)

Monday: (Mark 16:15)

_____

_____

_____

Tuesday: (Luke 24:52)

_____

_____

_____

Wednesday: (Acts 5:42)

_____

_____

_____

Thursday: (Ephesians 5:19-20)

_____

_____

_____

Friday: (Acts 15:19-20)

_____

_____

_____

Making it Personal: (Answer the following questions for personal reflection.)

1- Which of the three marks of Christ-like conduct in this lesson are your strengths?

Making it Practical: (Discuss the following questions with other members of your *Coaching with Impact* small group.)

1- Describe how the priorities of private worship and public worship look like in your life.

2- Read Luke 19:10. How did Jesus flesh out this priority of reaching the lost in His? How does it look in your life?

3- Read Acts 6:7. Are you reproducing or multiplying disciples in your life? Who do you know who is a true, reproducing disciple?

4- What happens when a church full of disciples is living out the conduct of Christ in its local community?

Making it Stick: (Do the following action step in the next week.) Look for an opportunity to have a "Christ-conversation" this week or an opportunity to invite someone to church.

Untrained Coaches to Fully Trained Coaches

By now you should have a clear understanding that Jesus came to make fully trained disciples who have His character and His conduct. When that happens with coaches, they make an impact on the athletes and other coaches they encounter.

The key is to understand that fully trained coaches don't happen by accident. No one just automatically becomes a fully trained disciple. A person moves from untrained to fully trained through a process. They take very intentional and strategic steps to move from untrained to fully trained.

Notice in Acts 4:13 Peter and John were described as *"uneducated, common men...that had been with Jesus"*. Now, go to Acts 17:6 and notice that Paul and Silas are described as, *"men who have turned the world upside down"*. The point here is that Jesus takes uneducated and untrained men and women and turns them into world changers!

The key to moving from untrained to fully trained is the phrase, *"with Jesus."* In Mark 3:14 we read, *"And he appointed twelve (whom he named apostles) so that they might be with him and that he might send them out to preach."* Jesus was very strategic in how he led these twelve men into a discipleship relationship. Let's take a look at how he did that so that we can do the same with the people God places in our lives.

Step One: "Come and See" Jesus intentionally invited people into a relationship by first taking the simple of step to come and see who He was and what He could do in their lives. In John 1:39 Jesus said to Andrew and Philip, *"Come and you will see."* Andrew and Philip were uneducated and common fishermen. They did not have seminary degrees or a formal biblical education but Jesus saw their potential to be world changers. In this initial step Jesus is not calling them to give up their lives, He is simply inviting them to discover who He is.

No one becomes a fully trained disciple without first taking a step to *"come and see"*. No coach becomes a world changing coach without first being invited to check out who Jesus is and what He can do. That leads me to this question: who in your life needs to get an invite from you? What coach or player needs you to invite them to "come and see" more about Jesus?

A coach who makes an impact is a coach who is consistently inviting people to "come and see" Jesus. It is a vital step in helping people move from untrained to fully trained.

Step Two: "Come and Follow" Jesus took those who came to see and He invited them to take a deeper step. He invited them to *"come and follow Him."* In John 1:43, Jesus said to Philip, *"follow Me."* With this invitation Jesus is actually asking these potential world changers to travel with Him and go from Bethany, near the Jordan, to Galilee. By foot, this trip would take days and during their travels they would begin to get to know each other. They would develop a relationship. They would experience community and learn much more about each other than they would from only spending one day together.

No one becomes a fully trained disciple without taking the step to *"come and follow."* A person must enter a relationship with Christ and His followers to ultimately grow into a world changer. The disciples of Jesus made a choice to follow Him and to connect with the other disciples. This small group would become the place where Jesus would train His disciples with His character and conduct. The relationship became the glue by which Jesus could equip these men to become disciples.

Who are the coaches or players that you need to invite into Christ-centered community? Who do you need to establish biblical community with that might eventually lead to a deeper commitment to learn and grow into Christ-likeness?

Step Three: "Come and Remain" As Jesus and the disciples experienced community He eventually called them to a deeper level of relationship. He called them to obedience. In John 8:31 Jesus said, *"If you abide in my word, you are truly my disciples."* To abide or remain in the word of Jesus is to obey what He says. Obedience is the sign or mark of a true disciple.

Jesus led his disciples from untrained to a point of training or equipping. At this point they are no longer simply seekers or followers, they are students. The Greek word for disciple is the word *"mathete"* which literally means to be trained or taught. Jesus made disciples that would become world changers by teaching them His character and conduct.

No one becomes a fully trained disciple without taking the step to *"come and remain"*. A person must be equipped and trained to become a fully trained disciple. They must be willing to obey Christ's words and do what He commanded them to do.

Step Four: "Come and Go" Jesus made disciples for the mission. He did not make disciples for the sake of simply making disciples. The goal of disciple making is never just to go deeper or to master spiritual disciplines. The goal of being a disciple is to be sent out. We "come and remain" so that we can "go" and make more disciples. In John 20:21 Jesus said, *"Peace be with you. As the father has sent me, even so I am sending you"*. Jesus made disciples in order to send out disciples.

In Matthew 28:19-20, Jesus told His disciples to, *"go make disciples of all nations."* He was sending them out to make disciples and to make disciples of every person, in every nation, in every generation. This mission has not changed in over two thousand years. It is the same mission today it was when Jesus commissioned his original disciples.

No one becomes a fully trained disciple without eventually going out and making more disciples. Fully trained disciples make more disciples by going, baptizing, and teaching others to obey what Christ commanded. They reproduce with others what has been done with them. This is how the movement of Christ multiplies and reaches "all nations".

Imagine what could happen if coaches all over the world were living "sent." What if every coach on ever team was looking for opportunities to reach people and teach people how to live and lead like Jesus? There could be an explosion of disciple making in the world if every coach saw themselves as being sent out to make more disciples.

So how about you? Are there some coaches or players that God is placing on your heart to lead through this course? Are you living "sent" and are you committed to fulfilling the mission of Jesus?

PUTTING IT ALL TOGETHER

A coach with impact is a coach who is reaching people for Christ. Helping them connect to community and eventually become a disciple who is becoming like Christ in character and conduct. When they are ready, the new disciple begins to reproduce the same process that they have experienced with others. Helping untrained coaches become fully trained coaches lasts for eternity! You have been put in the place you are to impact others for eternity and to help turn the world upside down.

WEEKLY WORK OUT: WEEK EIGHT

Main Takeaway: (Write down the one main takeaway you had from this week's lesson.)

_____

_____

_____

Memory Verse: (John 14:12)

_____

_____

_____

Meditation: (Write down your thoughts on the verse of the day.)

Monday: (Matthew 4:19)

_____

_____

_____

Tuesday: (Acts 1:8)

_____

_____

_____

Wednesday: (Luke 4:14-15)

_____

_____

_____

Thursday: (John 4:39)

_____

_____

_____

Friday: (Acts 9:31)

_____

_____

_____

Making it Personal: (Answer the following questions for personal reflection.)

1- Take a minute and evaluate your own journey through the steps of Jesus. What are observations come to mind?

Making it Practical: (Discuss the following questions with other members of your *Coaching with Impact* small group.)

1- Would you say Jesus was more strategic or more spontaneous in making disciples?

2- Read Acts 4:13 and Mark 3:14. What connections do you see, and how should we respond to those connections?

3- Discuss each of the four steps of how Jesus made disciples and why each is important.

4- Read Acts 17:6. Jesus made disciples for a purpose. What happens when the church is sending out fully trained disciples?

Making it Stick: (Do the following action step in the next week.) Write down the names of people you could currently help take each of the four steps in disciple making.

A Coach and The Word

Environment is everything! The environment we put ourselves in shapes who we are and what we do. That is exactly why Jesus used the environment of a small discipleship group to help transform His disciples. They developed the character and conduct of Christ by being in a small group where they encountered the Word of God, the Spirit of God, and the People of God.

The small group is still, two thousand years later, the ideal environment in which to make disciples. Jesus used the small group as a place to teach His disciples the Word of God. In fact, Jesus was the living word. John 1:14 says, *"And the Word became flesh and dwelt among us, and we have seen his glory, glory as of the only Son from the Father, full of grace and truth."*

The disciples had the living Word, Jesus, in their midst to learn from. Today we have the written Word, in our hands, to learn from. 2 Timothy 3:16,17 says, *"All scripture is breathed out by God and profitable for teaching, reproof, for correction, and for training in righteousness, that the man of God may be complete, equipped for every good work."*

When a group of coaches, players, or anybody for that matter, consistently meet together and open the Word of God together they will see the character and conduct of Christ taught all through the scriptures. As they consistently examine and expose themselves to the Word of God they will learn and know more and more of Christ's character and conduct. A person must have God's Word to know how to live and how to change.

Here is an example of how God's Word teaches us how we are to live. If you are reading Romans 10:14-17 you will discover that people can't believe in the gospel if they have not heard the message of Christ. That truth reminds you that we need to have the conduct of a "messenger" in the same way Jesus was a messenger. The Word of God teaches us how to live like the Son of God.

If you were reading in John 8 you would see a story about a woman caught in adultery. The way Jesus responds in this situation is a perfect example of His character on display. Jesus demonstrates "kindness" when the Pharisees were demonstrating condemnation. This picture of Christ's kindness is a great reminder of why our character needs to be more like Christ's.

You could actually read every passage in the Bible and question, "What does this passage teach me about Christ's character or conduct?" If you read the Bible that way, it will always speak to you, and even better, it can change you.

When a person continually exposes themselves to the Word of God they will realize how much they need Christ's character and conduct. You cannot understand Christ's character and conduct in a vacuum. God's Word is the written revelation for who are meant to be and what we need to do to live like the Son of God.

YOU NEED THE WORD

I once heard Pastor Rick Warren say, *"The more you get into God's Word, the more God's Word gets into you."* What a great truth! If you take that statement to the next level you could say that the more you get into God's Word the more you can have the character and conduct of Christ. It would also be true that the less you are in God's Word the less likely you are to have the character and conduct of Christ.

The goal, then, is to get into God's Word. Doing so is easier than you think. In fact, this course alone is helping you dig deeper into the Word of God. Here are some simple ways to get more of God's Word in you.

Memorize it! Psalm 119:11 says, *"I have stored up your word in my heart, that I might not sin against you."* Committing God's Word to memory is vital to your spiritual growth. As you put God's Word in your mind by memorizing it, you build a defense against sin and disobedience.

Read it! 1 Timothy 4:13 says, *"Until I come, devote yourself to the public reading of scripture, to exhortation, to teaching."* There is power in reading God's Word. Reading it with others and reading it alone are both ways of getting God's truth into your heart and mind.

Meditate on it! In Joshua 1:8 we read, *"This Book of the Law shall not depart from your mouth, but you shall meditate on it day and night, so that you may be careful to do according to all that's written in it."* Meditating on God's Word simply means thinking about what you read and asking questions about it. Rather than quickly reading over a verse, meditation means taking the time to think about what it says and means.

Study it! Psalm 119:18 says, *"Open my eyes, that I may behold wondrous things out of your law."* When you study or examine God's Word you discover wondrous things about God. When you study the scriptures, God opens your eyes and reveals to you who He is and what He desires of you. Studying God's word involves observation, interpretation, and application. All of these steps help to open your eyes to what God is trying to show you.

Listen to it! In Ezra 7:10 the Bible says, *"For Ezra had set his heart to study the Law of the Lord, and to do it and to teach his statutes and rules in Israel."* God gave his people a teacher to communicate and teach them the truth of his Word. We can learn more of God's Word when we listen to it taught by called and gifted teachers.

COACHES IN GOD'S WORD

As you work through *Coaching with Impact* you will be encouraged and challenged to grow in God's Word. The lessons, memory verses, and daily scriptures meditations will help you get into God's Word. As you get into the Word of God you will become more like the Son of God. If that happens, we have accomplished our goal to help you become a fully trained coach.

WEEKLY WORK OUT: WEEK NINE

Main Takeaway: (Write down the one main takeaway you had from this week's lesson.)

_____

_____

_____

Memory Verse: (Psalm 119:105)

_____

_____

_____

Meditation: (Write down your thoughts on the verse of the day.)

Monday: (Proverbs 30:5)

_____

_____

_____

Tuesday: (Ephesians 6:17)

_____

_____

_____

Wednesday: (2 Peter 1:20)

_____

_____

_____

Thursday: (1 Corinthians 2:5)

_____

_____

_____

Friday: (Psalm 119:103)

_____

_____

_____

Making it Personal: (Answer the following questions for personal reflection.)

1- Are you studying God's Word currently?

Making it Practical: (Discuss the following questions with other members of your *Coaching with Impact* small group.)

1- How are you "growing in God's Word" right now?

2- Read 2 Timothy 3:16-17. Share an example of how God's Word has taught, reproofed, corrected, or trained you in some way.

3- Describe how the Word of God and Spirit of God work together to make you more like the Son of God.

4- Read Ezra 7:10. How does your attitude toward God's Word compare to that of Ezra?

Making it Stick: (Do the following action step in the next week.) Read Mark, chapter 1, and write down any observations (what it says), any interpretations (what it means), and some applications (how it applies).

A Coach and The Spirit

When the Spirit of God intersects with the Word of God in a person's life, transformation can happen. When someone is seeing the need to live as a "servant" while reading God's Word, and the Holy Spirit is leading them to do an act of service for a person in need, that creates "life change." That type of process happening over and over again for a lifetime is how a person lives a life of impact.

God's Word + God's Spirit= Transformation

The presence of God's Spirit in the life of a disciple is essential for living out the character and conduct of Christ. In fact, it is impossible to live out the life of Christ in your own strength and power. Christ wants to live His life through you as a result of the Spirit's filling and leading.

Jesus actually promised to send His Spirit so that His disciples (and all of us) could have the power we need to live for Him. In John 14:16,17 Jesus said, *"And I will ask the Father, and he will give you another helper, to be with you forever, even the Spirit of truth, whom the world cannot receive, because it neither sees him or knows him. You know him, for he dwells with you and will be in you."* The Holy Spirit is the presence of God inside your life. When Jesus left the planet, He could no longer speak to his disciples so He sent His Spirit. With the Spirit, Jesus can be with everyone, all the time. The Spirit can remind you of what Jesus taught and bring it to your mind exactly when you need it. John 14:26 says, *"But the Helper, the Holy Spirit, whom the Father will send in My Name, He will teach you all things and bring to remembrance all that I have said to you."*

What an awesome thing that God lives in the believer through the presence of his Spirit and as you yield your will to his control he gives you the power to do what his word instructs you to do. A coach who is living a life yielded to the control of the Holy Spirit is one who is able to demonstrate the character and conduct of Christ, not because of their self effort, but because of the indwelling presence of the Holy Spirit.

THE SPIRIT-CONTROLLED COACH

When you give your life to Christ the Holy Spirit takes up residence inside you. Once the Holy Spirit is in you, He wants to empower you and lead you. As you yield your will to His will, it allows the Holy Spirit to lead you and empower you to live the life Christ wants you to live.

Being yielded to the Holy Spirit is a moment by moment choice to surrender control of your life to Him. The Holy Spirit will never override your will. He will never force you or control you without your allowing Him. Paul described it this way in Galatians 5:16, *"But I say, walk by the Spirit, and you will not gratify the desires of the flesh."* When you walk you do so one step at a time. When you walk by the Spirit you do the same thing. Moment by moment you allow the Holy Spirit to have control and direct your path.

As you walk in the Spirit, He is constantly reminding you of Christ's character. You may find yourself in a stressful situation where God reminds you of His peace and patience. Walking in the Spirit can also remind you of Christ's conduct. God might allow your path to cross with someone far from God and the Spirit reminds you to be a witness or messenger of the gospel. Walking in the Spirit is the most exciting way to live. You never know when God is going to allow His Word and your circumstances to intersect and give you an opportunity to respond in a Christlike manner.

If you keep filling your mind with the Word of God and keep walking in step with the Spirit of God you will soon begin to respond more and more like the Son of God. This is the victorious Christian life. Instead of allowing your circumstances and situations to control you, you are allowing the Holy Spirit to control you regardless of the circumstance.

EXPERIENCING VICTORY

The coach who is walking in the Spirit and living above his or her circumstances is the coach who truly has victory in life. Paul says in Ephesians 5:18, *"And do not get drunk with wine, for that is debauchery, but be filled with the Spirit"*. Alcohol alters a persons' behavior and attitude. It can cause a person to be and do what they might not normally be or do. Being filled with God's Spirit can also alter a person. The Holy Spirit can change your attitude and behavior and make you more like Christ's when you are filled with the Spirit.

If a coach is walking in the Spirit and they find themselves in a situation that might cause them to be angry the Spirit can remind them of love, goodness, and kindness. At that moment they can submit to the Spirit's control and choose to respond without anger. Boom, that's victory! Always remember, no one can make you angry, frustrated, or impatient without your permission. You only give in to your circumstances because you choose not to let the Spirit of Christ inside you to have control.

WHAT THE WORLD NEEDS

Can you see now why the world needs Spirit-controlled coaches? Can you see how differently athletics would be when coaches and players respond from a posture of Spirit control rather than fleshly or worldly control? Teamwork, competition, and sportsmanship are all demonstrated differently when coaches and players are operating out of a Spirit-controlled life.

We need coaches who are becoming fully trained disciples who demonstrate the character and conduct of Christ. Coaches who operate our of a Spirit-filled life rather than a flesh-controlled life. Coaches who have a different manner about them. Coaches who don't blow their cool, berate their players, and stay in conflict with other coaches. We need coaches who maintain composure in the heat of competition, treat players and other coaches appropriately, and remain calm under pressure. We need Spirit-controlled coaches.

If you have given your life to Christ, His Spirit dwells within you and desires to empower you. Ask the Holy Spirit to fill you and to have His way in you. Yield your will to His will and He will have His way in your life.

WEEKLY WORK OUT: WEEK TEN

Main Takeaway: (Write down the one main takeaway you had from this week's lesson.)

_____

_____

_____

Memory Verse: (Romans 7:9)

_____

_____

_____

Meditation: (Write down your thoughts on the verse of the day.)

Monday: (1 Corinthians 6:19)

_____

_____

_____

Tuesday: (John 16:13)

_____

_____

_____

Wednesday: (Romans 8:9)

_____

_____

_____

Thursday: (Zechariah 4:6)

_____

_____

_____

Friday: (1 Corinthians 2:14)

_____

_____

_____

Making it Personal: (Answer the following questions for personal reflection.)

1- Are you living your life under the control and influence of the Spirit or under the control of your "self"?

Making it Practical: (Discuss the following questions with other members of your *Coaching with Impact* small group.)

1- Describe the differences between a Spirit-controlled coach and a self-controlled coach.

2- Read Galatians 5:16. What does it mean to "walk by the Spirit"? How does that connect with Ephesians 5:18?

3- How much of you does the Holy Spirit "have" right now?

4- Read John 14:26 and share an example of how the Holy Spirit has reminded you of something Jesus taught.

Making it Stick: (Do the following action step in the next week.) Take some time and journal areas in your life where the Holy Spirit is speaking to you, and if needed, take in those areas.

A Coach and The People of God

When a person is growing in the Word of God, living controlled by the Spirit of God, and being surrounded by the People of God they are in position to become more like the Son of God. This combination is how people have become fully trained disciples for the last two thousand plus years. It worked with Jesus and His disciples and it will work with you.

Most people underestimate the role that God's people play in the disciple making process. Jesus did not make disciples in isolation, He made them in the context of relationships. The whole group of disciples was instrumental in the making of each individual disciple. When Jesus called the twelve he knew they not only needed to be with Him, He knew they needed to be with each other.

God's Word + God's Spirit + God's People = Transformation

If it were up to me, I probably would not pick other people to be a part of the disciple making process. But that's why God is God and I'm not. Only God could create a plan where He would use other people to help people become more like Him. Only God could devise a plan where the interaction between disciples would be strategic part of helping people become fully trained disciples.

Coaches need other coaches to help them become fully trained disciples. Hopefully, you are doing this course in the context of a small group of other coaches. If so, you already understand why this is so critical to the disciple making process. You can become a coach with impact if you are growing in the Word of God, controlled by the Spirit of God, and surrounded by the People of God.

God's Word teaches you what the character and conduct of Christ looks like. God's Spirit empowers and leads you to obey God's Word. God's People encourage you and come alongside you to help you do what the Holy Spirit is leading you to do.

BETTER TOGETHER

Every coach knows the importance of team. Teams work together for a common goal. They encourage each other. They support each other. They hold each other accountable and they challenge each other. There are lots of great advantages to working together as a team.

Ecclesiastes 4:9-12 is a great reminder of how we can accomplish more together than on our own: *"Two are better than one, because they have a good reward for their toil. For if they fall, one will lift up his fellow. But woe to him who is alone when he falls and has not another to lift him up! Again, if two lie together, they keep warm, but how can one keep warm alone? And though a man might prevail against one who is alone, two will withstand him- a threefold cord is not quickly broken."*

Obviously God knows the importance of team as well. When we surround ourselves with the People of God we have people to help us when we fall, to protect us when attacked, and to give us strength when we are weak. Even better is a team that has Christ in the center. The three fold cord is exponentially stronger than a two fold cord. When you have coaches working together with Christ in the center you have a powerful team.

As you meet with other coaches each week to work through *Coaching With Impact* you are positioning yourself to grow and become a fully trained disciple. The other coaches can speak into your life as the Word of God and the Spirit of God are leading you to become more like the Son of God. Hopefully you are experiencing some of the advantages of a small group as you work on becoming a fully trained disciple.

Accountability! Having a partner to work out or run with provides me with healthy accountability. I am more likely to show up and do what I need to do because someone else is doing it with me. Proverbs 27:17 says, *"Iron sharpens iron, and one man sharpens another".* When I have other disciples in my life I am much more likely to read my bible, pray, and share my faith. Other disciples make me sharper!

Encouragement! Hebrews 10:25 says, *"Not neglecting to meet together, as some are in the habit of doing, but encourage one another, and all the more as you see the Day drawing near".* When a small group of coaches meet together each week it provides an opportunity to encourage each other. We live in a world where you can never have too much encouragement. It needs to become a habit in our lives.

Prayer! Praying for each other and with each other is an important part of what happens in a small discipleship group. Praying together unites us and gives us strength as we face the trials of life. The disciples in the upper room were praying together as they sought God's guidance following Christ's crucifixion and resurrection. Filled with fear, the disciples gained strength by praying with each other. The church was actually birthed out of that upper room prayer meeting. There is great power when coaches gather together to pray with and for each other.

HOW ALL WORKS TOGETHER

Let's take a minute and look at how the Word of God, Spirit of God, and People of God all work together to make us more like the Son of God.

If my goal is to become a fully trained coach, I will make the commitment to study God's Word and allow it to shape my character and conduct to be more like Christ. As I live surrendered to the Spirit of God He shows me people and places where I need to adjust and change to be more like Christ. As I meet weekly with other Christian coaches, the People of God help me live out what the Word and Spirit are leading me to do through encouragement, accountability and prayer. God uses this combination to bring about transformation and make me more like Jesus.

The key to this whole process is consistency. The disciples were with Jesus for approximately three years. When you dedicate yourself to a small discipleship group for an extended period of time it gives God an opportunity to change your life and make you into a world changer. Who wouldn't want to be part of a process like that?

WEEKLY WORK OUT: WEEK ELEVEN

Main Takeaway: (Write down the one main takeaway you had from this week's lesson.)

_____

_____

_____

Memory Verse: (Ephesians 4:32)

_____

_____

_____

Meditation: (Write down your thoughts on the verse of the day.)

Monday: (Acts 1:14)

_____

_____

_____

Tuesday: (Acts 4:32)

_____

_____

_____

Wednesday: (Romans 13:8)

_____

_____

_____

Thursday: (1 Corinthians 13:11)

_____

_____

_____

Friday: (Ephesians 4:16)

_____

_____

_____

Making it Personal: (Answer the following questions for personal reflection.)

1- Do you have good people in your life and are you allowing them to encourage you as you become more like Jesus?

Making it Practical: (Discuss the following questions with other members of your *Coaching with Impact* small group.)

1- Is it important to be surrounded by people who encourage you in your walk with God? Why or why not?

2- Read Ecclesiastes 4:9-12. What are the benefits of being in a small group versus not being in a group?

3- How are you doing at giving other people accountability, encouragement, and prayer?

4- Read Ephesians 4:16. How can other believers, God's Spirit, and God's Word create transformation in someone's life?

Making it Stick: (Do the following action step in the next week.) Reach out to someone in your life or small group and encourage them in someone way this next week.

Becoming A Coach Who Multiplies Disciples

Congratulations! You are about to complete the *Coaching With Impact* course... or are you? The truth is, you have actually just begun being a Coach With Impact. The real impact of your position as a coach starts now. What you do now that you have finished this study is incredibly important. I would hate to think that you have worked your way through this book on being and building disciples and simply put the book on the shelf to think about it no more. If that is the case, you will have missed what this entire course is intended to accomplish.

The past eleven weeks have been designed to help you understand what it means to be a fully trained coach so that now you can turn around and reproduce the concept in other coaches. When that happens a movement of multiplication has begun.

Just think about this for a moment. God did not put you in the role of a coach by accident. He did not give you the influence you have just to win ball games! He put you there to influence people. God has strategically placed you where you are in the world to influence other coaches and players for the sake of Jesus. As my friend and baseball scout, Kevin Burrell, says, "I'm a disciple maker disguised as a baseball scout." That's 100% true! Kevin works as a professional baseball scout, but his real reason for being on the planet is to make disciples who make disciples.

He just happens to get paid to find great baseball players while he makes disciples. What a great gig.

Remember also that you did not wind up in this *Coaching With Impact* group by accident. God orchestrated events and people in a way that got you connected to this group so that in turn you would lead a group at some point. That may mean now or it may mean later. It does mean sometime.

YOU'VE BEEN DISCIPLED TO BUILD DISCIPLES

Jesus did not make disciples so they could stay in a holy huddle until He returned. Jesus made disciples so that until He returned they would repeat the process with as many people as possible.

You have been led through *Coaching With Impact* so that at some point you could led someone else through it. The question is when are you ready to lead someone else?

The Bible clearly emphasizes the importance of spiritual leaders being qualified before leading. The same is true with *Coaching with Impact*. The fact that you have completed the course does not necessarily mean you are ready to lead someone else through the course. At least not yet!

The best person to help you discern whether or not you are spiritually qualified to lead someone else is the person who led you. Your group leader can help you discern if you are ready to lead a group or if you need to co-lead a group before leading on your own. Even Jesus sent His disciples out in pairs, so being a co-leader is actually an important part of multiplying disciples.

If you are a new believer it would probably be best if you serve as a co-leader with a more mature leader. If you have never really grown as a believer it might be best too co-lead for a while. If you do not feel like you truly demonstrate the character and conduct of Christ then it might be best to co-lead for while. If you are a little uneasy taking the lead of a group it might be best to co-lead with someone.

If none of the above apply to you then it is time to get busy and start leading a group of coaches. Ask the Lord to show you who you need to invite to a group and get started once He leads you to the right coaches. Luke 6:12 tells us what Jesus did before choosing His disciples, *"...went out to the mountain to pray, and all night he continued in prayer to God."* If we are smart we will follow Christ's example and pray about the people we will invest our lives in.

QUALIFICATIONS OF A LEADER

When it comes to being a leader you will want to look for someone who is spiritually qualified. You will want to look for someone who has a good understanding of the basics of faith, but also someone that demonstrates the character and conduct of Christ. This course will provide some of what it means to have Christ-like character and conduct, but the goal is to see it being lived out in the life of a potential leader. Do not put a person into spiritual leadership too soon. Be sure they are ready before they are held accountable to teach and lead others.

QUALIFICATIONS OF A DISCIPLE

When it comes to finding someone to be in your group as a disciple there are some things to look for as well. First, look for someone who is faithful. You want to invest in people who will show and up and do what is expected of them. Also, look for people who are hungry and ready to grow. You want to invest in people with a genuine desire for more and not doing so out of obligation or to get someone else off their back. You will also want to find a person who has a teachable spirit. A person who is a know-it-all is not someone you can make much progress with. Look for the person with the right attitude about growing and learning.

INCREDIBLE POTENTIAL

I hope you are grasping what can happen through this *Coaching With Impact* course. If not, let me leave you with a few thoughts about what could happen if a handful of coaches embrace the idea of being coaches with impact.

First, lots of coaches will be transformed. If only three coaches discover the character and conduct of Christ, that will be three coaches who are different because of this effort. Only God knows who those three coaches might impact. If three hundred or three thousand coaches discover the character and conduct of Christ, that will have a huge impact on the world around them. Thousands of people could be changed by the faithfulness of coaches who are fully trained disciples. Only God can see the reach of an effort like *Coaching with Impact*.

Second, a movement could begin. If a handful of coaches decided to disciple more coaches it could start a ripple that could last a long time and reach many. Wouldn't it be incredible to see a revival like this take place among coaches? Only God can see the extent of the potential impact if a few coaches get serious about discipling more coaches.

Third, we put a dent in the darkness. Disciple making is the ideal way to reach the world. If you had a movement of coaches who are demonstrating Christlike character and conduct, imagine how many more people might come to faith in Jesus and begin to grow in Him. This is exactly why Jesus chose disciple making as the means to reach "all nations."

Twelve weeks could have a powerful outcome. All that needs to happen is to have a few coaches commit to the process of making more disciples. God has given us the power and He has given us the plan. All that is needed now is obedience. Will you obey what Jesus has called you to do?

WEEKLY WORK OUT: WEEK TWELVE

Main Takeaway: (Write down the one main takeaway you had from this week's lesson.)

_____

_____

_____

Memory Verse: (Acts 6:7)

_____

_____

_____

Meditation: (Write down your thoughts on the verse of the day.)

Monday: (1 Thessalonians 1:6)

_____

_____

_____

Tuesday: (2 Timothy 2:2)

_____

_____

_____

Wednesday: (Acts 14:21-22)

_____

_____

_____

Thursday: (Psalm 78:4)

_____

_____

_____

Friday: (Matthew 16:24)

_____

_____

_____

Making it Personal: (Answer the following questions for personal reflection.)

1- How do you feel about the possibility of leading someone else through *Coaching with Impact*?

Making it Practical: (Discuss the following questions with other members of your *Coaching with Impact* small group.)

1- How would you describe what this course has meant to you over the past few months?

2- Why is disciple making among coaches such an important concept?

3- What are some of the barriers that could inhibit the multiplication disciples in the sports world?

4- Now that you've completed *Coaching with Impact,* what is the next step for you in disciple making?

Making it Stick: (Do the following action step in the next week.) Have a conversation with your group leader about the possibility of leading a *Coaching with Impact* group or helping someone else lead a group as an assistant leader. You may also consider using the funnel on the following page as a strategy for taking disconnected, untrained people and developing them into fully trained disciples of Jesus if you do lead a group.

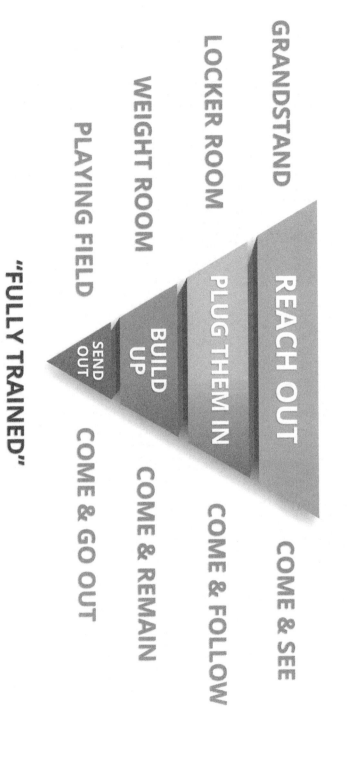

"DISCONNECTED"

GRANDSTAND

LOCKER ROOM

WEIGHT ROOM

PLAYING FIELD

"FULLY TRAINED"

REACH OUT

PLUG THEM IN

BUILD UP

SEND OUT

COME & SEE

COME & FOLLOW

COME & REMAIN

COME & GO OUT

LEARN MORE

We have other great book studies, free resources, blogs, podcasts, and more available at impactdisciples.com.

   @ImpactDiscipleship

   @ImpactDisciples

Made in the USA
Columbia, SC
29 July 2022

64311708R00055